bake me I'm yours...
cupcake

Joan and Graham Belgrove

D&C
David and Charles

We would like to dedicate this book to:

Bessie, George, Edna and Frank

A DAVID & CHARLES BOOK
Copyright © David & Charles Limited
2007, 2010

David & Charles is an F+W Media Inc. company
4700 East Galbraith Road
Cincinnati, OH 45236

First published in 2007
This paperback edition first published in the UK
in 2010
Reprinted in 2009 (four times), 2010

Text and designs copyright © Joan and
Graham Belgrove 2007, 2010
Photography copyright David & Charles
2007, 2010

Joan and Graham Belgrove have asserted their
right to be identified as author of this work in
accordance with the Copyright, Designs and
Patents Act, 1988.

Names of manufacturers and other products
are provided for the information of readers,
with no intention to infringe copyright or
trademarks.

A catalogue record for this book is available
from the British Library.

ISBN-13: 978-0-7153-3762-2 paperback
ISBN-10: 0-7153-3762-9 paperback

Printed in China by Toppan Leefung
Printing Limited
for David & Charles
Brunel House   Newton Abbot   Devon

Commissioning Editor Jennifer Fox-Proverbs
Desk Editor Bethany Dymond
Head of design Prudence Rogers
Art Editor Sarah Underhill
Designer Emma Sandquest
Project Editor Natasha Reed
Production Controller Kelly Smith
Photographer Lorna Yabsley

David & Charles publish high quality books
on a wide range of subjects.
For more great book ideas visit:
www.rucraft.co.uk

Contents

cupcake heaven...

Cupcakes are now becoming so popular that they are establishing themselves in many new ways – people are, for instance, sending cupcakes instead of flowers, bringing a box full of cupcakes to a party instead of a bottle, having champagne and cupcakes parties, and celebrating all kinds of special occasions, from Baby Showers to Diamond Weddings, with cupcakes. Cupcake tiers are now the new fashion in wedding cakes too.

Cupcakes are without doubt 'a cake for all seasons' – universally appreciated by young and old – and so versatile – truly there's a cupcake design for every occasion. You certainly don't need an excuse to indulge in a cupcake, but there are so many occasions at any time of year to celebrate, so why not make the most of them by creating innovative cupcake designs. This book shows you clever ways – some quick, some more detailed – to decorate your cupcakes to turn them into cakes fit for the funkiest teen, poshest wedding, laziest picnic or any special occasion imaginable.

All you need to know is in here – it is full of ideas which hopefully will inspire you to create your own cupcake designs for whatever the occasion or celebration... and have fun in the process. We hope you will enjoy the pages that follow and more importantly have a go and join in the fun!

bake me...

This section is about mixing and baking the sponge itself. After all, you have to bake the cakes before you can get on with the fun part of creating designs! Read this part thoroughly and make sure have all the materials and equipment to hand before you begin.

Basic Equipment...

- ♡ Food processor or hand-held whisk
- ♡ Food mixer or hand-held mixer
- ♡ Spatula
- ♡ Measuring spoons
- ♡ Cooling racks
- ♡ Baking tray
- ♡ Sieve

what you'll need

We'll take it as read that you've got a cooker, refrigerator, kitchen sink etc – so here are the other basics. Food mixing can be done either by machine or by hand if you don't have an electric mixer.

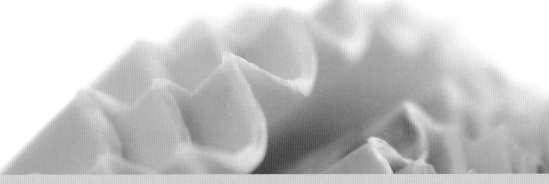

baking cases and trays

There is a variety of different sizes to choose from, which allows you to try different looks and designs when creating your cupcake masterpieces.

Throughout the book, we use four different sizes of cupcakes:
Very Little – petit four case
Little – a mini muffin case size, 31mm (1 1/8in) x 23mm (1in)

Not So Little – a traditional fairy cake case, 45mm (1¾in) x 27mm (1 1/16in)
Not At All Little – traditional muffin case

Baking trays for cupcakes are usually either 12 or 24 cup. Make sure you purchase the right size tray to fit the cake cases snugly.

Fill the paper cases about half full with the cupcake mixture, allowing plenty of room for your cakes to rise to perfection.

You will know when to take your cakes out of the oven, as the centre will spring back when touched. Leave the cupcakes to cool in the baking tray for five minutes then transfer to a cooling rack to cool completely and enjoy!

size matters

Each sponge recipe should make one batch of:
48 'Very Little' cupcakes with a few over
36 'Little' with a few over
24 'Not So Little' cupcakes with a few over, or
12 'Not At All Little' cupcakes with a few over.

Check out the 'flavour me' ideas opposite for delicious alternatives to the basic vanilla sponge.

vanilla sponge

1 Pre-heat the oven to 175°C/347°F/ Gas 4. Place cases in bun trays.

2 Put sugar, then flour (sieved), then chopped up butter and vanilla extract into a food processor. Blitz all together on medium power until well mixed together. Alternatively mix it all together with a hand-held whisk.

3 Then add eggs one by one, using a slow pulse setting, if using a food processor, until the mix is integrated.

ingredients...

♡ 225g (8oz) slightly salted butter

♡ 225g (8oz) caster sugar

♡ 4 medium eggs

♡ 225g (8oz) self-raising flour

♡ 5ml (1 tsp) natural vanilla extract

The mixture should be a soft dropping consistency when ready to spoon out into baking cases.

4 Spoon the mixture into the cases, and place in the baking tray. Place in the centre of the oven and bake for:
11–12 minutes ('Very Little')
13–14 minutes ('Little')
15–17 minutes ('Not So Little')
18–20 minutes ('Not At All Little')
Bake for the time mentioned or until the tops of the cakes spring back when lightly touched.

5 Turn out and cool on wire racks.

chocolate sponge

1 Pre-heat the oven to 170°C/338°F/ Gas 3–4. Place cases in bun trays.

2 Put sugar, butter, eggs and vanilla extract into food processor. Blitz together on full power for a good 2–3 minutes. Remove blade. Alternatively, mix it all together with a hand-held whisk.

3 Sieve the flour, baking powder and cocoa together into a separate bowl and then add to the mix gradually, folding in with a spatula.

ingredients...

- ♡ 3 medium eggs
- ♡ 175g (6oz) caster sugar
- ♡ 115g (4oz) self-raising flour
- ♡ 30ml (6 tsp) cocoa powder
- ♡ 7.5ml (1.5 tsp) baking powder
- ♡ 5ml (1 tsp) natural vanilla extract
- ♡ 175g (6oz) slightly salted butter

Use the best quality cocoa you can find, ideally Dutch-processed cocoa.

If you are short of time you can buy plain cupcakes from the supermarket or bakery, ready to decorate.

4 Spoon the mixture into the baking cases.

5 Place in the centre of the oven and bake for:
12–13 minutes ('Very Little')
14–15 minutes ('Little')
16–18 minutes ('Not So Little')
20–22 minutes ('Not At All Little')
Bake for the time mentioned or until the tops of the cakes spring back when lightly touched.

6 Turn out and cool on wire racks.

flavour me...
Try these other flavours for tasty variations in cupcakes.

coffee sponge
Use the basic vanilla sponge recipe but add in 1 tablespoon of strong instant coffee dissolved in 1 tablespoon of milk and pulse into the mix at the very end.

orange & lemon
Just substitute orange or lemon for vanilla extract in the basic sponge recipe.

lavender
This flavour would work very well for a unique cupcake.

frost me...

The next stage is adding the icing or frosting to your cupcakes. With a little practice, it is easy to achieve a professional-looking iced or frosted finish. None of the projects in this book require any great expertise. If you can roll out pastry and cut out shapes you will soon do everything else with a bit of practice.

basic equipment...

♡ Smooth non-stick board

♡ Rolling pin

♡ Flexible plastic spatulas

♡ Piping bags

♡ Nozzles of various shapes

♡ Palette knives

♡ Sieve

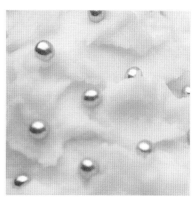

flavour me...

Any of the icing and frosting recipes that follow can be easily adapted.

get fruity

fruity essences such as lemon and orange add a delicate hint of flavour and are especially perfect for spring and summer creations.

get fresh

Peppermint essence gives a delicious freshness, while rose essence adds a taste of romance.

to get the taste...

Just substitute some of the water (or vanilla extract if buttercream) with the flavouring.

frosting

This is the general term used to describe a smooth, creamy style of icing, achieved by the addition and blending in of butter.

buttercream frosting

1 Beat the butter until soft in a food processor. Alternatively use a hand-held whisk.

2 Gradually beat in the icing sugar and water together.

3 Continue beating until frosting is light and fluffy.

4 Towards the end add the vanilla extract.

ingredients...

♡ 225g (8oz) unsalted butter

♡ 5ml (1 tsp) natural vanilla extract

♡ 450g (1lb) sifted icing sugar

♡ 40 ml (2½ tbsp) cold water

chocolate buttercream frosting

1 Sift the cocoa together with the icing sugar.

2 Beat the butter to a cream in a food mixer. Alternatively use a hand-held whisk.

3 Add water and icing/cocoa, mixing together gradually while beating.

Coffee or chocolate flavouring can also be easily made by dissolving either instant coffee powder or cocoa in hot water and mixing together with the icing.

ingredients...

- ♡ 175g (6oz) sifted icing sugar
- ♡ 50g (2oz) cocoa, Dutch processed if possible
- ♡ 45ml (3 tbsp) cold water
- ♡ 115g (4oz) soft unsalted butter

royal icing

Royal Icing distinguishes itself from other icing by its pure white, smooth finish that can be achieved. This is the best icing to use for piping work on your cakes. Royal icing is now widely available to buy as a ready mix, to which you just add hot water. If, however, you want to make your own here is the recipe.

ingredients...

♡ white of 1 medium egg

♡ 225g (8oz) sifted icing sugar

♡ 2–3 drops of lemon juice

1 Beat egg white until foamy.

2 Gradually beat in icing sugar and lemon juice, and continue beating for five minutes until icing is snowy white.

It is best to use royal icing as soon as it is made because it sets and hardens fairly quickly. If this is not possible, keep the icing covered with a damp cloth until ready for use.

fondant icing

There are two types of fondant icing; pouring and ready to roll (see bottom of page). This is the recipe for both.

1 Follow the method for royal icing. **For pouring fondant** you will need a spreading consistency; but the fondant should not be too thin, as it will run too fast to the edges of the cupcake.

For ready to roll fondant, make a paste or dough by adding a greater quantity of icing sugar and kneading on a board dusted with icing sugar for 10 minutes.

2 Cover with a clean cloth and leave for half an hour before using.

ingredients...

♡ 225g (8oz) sifted icing sugar (plus extra if making ready to roll fondant)

♡ 2–3 tablespoons liquid glucose

♡ white of 1 medium egg

For an even finish when applying pouring fondant, smooth out the icing with a flat bladed knife that has been wetted and excess water shaken off.

pouring fondant

When used as a pouring fondant, this icing gives a better, smoother, satin finish to the tops of cupcakes, when compared to, say, glacé icing, which is simply icing sugar mixed with hot water. It is now becoming widely available to purchase as a packet mix, but we have also included the recipe above.

ready to roll fondant

This is the same as pouring fondant icing but made thicker and kneaded into a paste or dough. We, however, have chosen to use ready-made rolled fondant (sometimes called Regal Ice) in this book.

petal paste

This, in simple terms, is just like ready to roll fondant but hardens quickly and is useful as a modelling paste for making delicate shapes. Petal paste, sometimes referred to as sugar florist paste or modelling paste, can of course be made from scratch but we would recommend the ready-made products for their convenience.

ingredients...

- ♥ 225g (8oz) sifted icing sugar
- ♥ 10–15ml (2–3 tbsp) liquid glucose
- ♥ 15ml (1 tbsp) powdered gelatine
- ♥ 5ml (1tsp) glycerine
- ♥ 1 egg white

1 To make, follow the method for royal icing and then knead on a board dusted with cornflour for 10 minutes. Icing sugar can tend to dry the petal paste out too much if used on the rolling pin and board.

2 Add more icing sugar if necessary to get the consistency of a dough. To get a really smooth, flat, round disc of icing on top of your cupcake, make sure cupcakes are really cooled and, if the cake is rounded on top, shave the centre flat with a sharp knife.

Colouring for icing and frosting is available in various forms – e.g. liquid and paste. Use a cocktail stick to add a little colour at a time so you don't overdo it.

adorn me...

Decorating your cakes can be really simple by just adding a variety of different embellishments, as the projects throughout the book show.

decorations and embellishments

Having a large stock of different sprinkles, sparkles and novelty toppings is the key to cupcake making! Although there is a huge variety in your local supermarket and specialist shops, use the internet for further choice. There's an incredible range to choose from and you don't have to buy huge quantities to get hold of them.

fake it...

Embellishments don't always have to be edible. Candles, cocktail umbrellas, miniature statues and other items can be used to turn your cupcake into a work of art. Be careful with non-edible items when serving the cakes; make sure no children can choke on small objects or knock candles over to start a fire.

Some of the techniques in the book call for a bit of patience and precision. But if that's not for you – do your own thing.

Plan ahead in order to co-ordinate the colours of the icings, frostings and sprinkles – whether it's a pastel theme or a snazzy, glitzy theme.

When adding sweets or embellishments to cupcakes, it is best if the icing has set slightly but is still tacky enough to make sure the topping won't fall off.

Sprinkles don't have to be applied individually – just pour a lot of them into a shallow dish and then tip your cupcakes upside down onto them.

case study

Cupcake cases, whilst they might not seem too important, are a big part of your cake design. Just like decorations, the right case can make or break the look of your cake. There is a huge variety of cases available, from themed seasonal cases, to glitzy gold or silver foil cases. So take the time to hunt around for a case which will suit the theme you are aiming for with the cupcake design.

eat me...

romantic moments

i ♡ valentine

Roses are red, violets are blue, but if cupcakes always do it for you… just enjoy!
These vanilla cupcakes are sweet in more ways than one with delicious
buttercream frosting and delicate heart motifs.

for 36 cakes...

- ♡ 1 batch of Little vanilla cupcakes in red foil cases
- ♡ ½ batch of buttercream frosting
- ♡ ½ batch of royal icing
- ♡ thin nozzled piping bag
- ♡ greaseproof paper

1 Make the hearts the night before. Keeping the line continuous, pipe out heart shapes onto greaseproof paper with the royal icing, and leave to set.

2 Carefully peel off in the morning and leave on a flat clean surface until ready to use.

3 Pipe a generous swirl of buttercream frosting onto the cupcakes and gently push the heart shapes into position.

lovers' tip
If you haven't time to pipe the hearts then just make the hearts out of petal paste and cut out with a heart-shaped cutter (right).

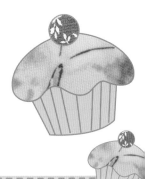

back to basics vanilla cupcakes p8... buttercream frosting p12... royal icing p14...

come in for coffee

All dark and sultry – an irresistible combination of moist rich chocolate cake with a two tone coffee and chocolate frosting, topped with a chocolate-coated coffee bean… who needs after dinner mints when you've got these!

for 36 cakes...

- ♡ 1 batch of Little chocolate cupcakes in black foil cases
- ♡ 1 batch of frosting, divided to make chocolate and coffee flavoured
- ♡ large star nozzled piping bag
- ♡ chocolate-coated coffee beans
- ♡ cocoa powder

1 Pipe the chocolate frosting in a large swirl all over the cakes; then apply a smaller swirl of coffee frosting onto the centre of each cake, using a similar nozzle head.

2 Gently push a couple of the coated coffee beans into the middle, just enough to secure them.

3 Finish with a light dusting of cocoa powder – just like on a cappuccino.

a dark secret
Put a generous splash of Tia Maria or Kahlua in when you are making the frosting – wicked!

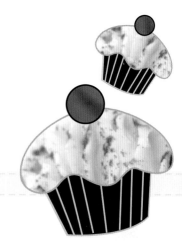

back to basics chocolate cupcakes p9... frosting p13...

love is in the air

Spring, that time of year when one's thoughts turn to... cupcakes, of course!
A light, refreshing mix of pastel colours, conjuring up all things fresh and new.
The sweet butterflies add a feminine touch to these cakes.

for 24 cakes...

- ♡ 1 batch of Not So Little vanilla cupcakes in pastel pink cases
- ♡ 1 batch of pink fondant icing
- ♡ small quantity of royal icing, coloured pink
- ♡ small silver balls for decoration
- ♡ coloured petal paste
- ♡ small nozzled piping bag
- ♡ small heart-shaped cutters, in two sizes

1 Carefully cover each cupcake with a cap of pink fondant icing. Take care to get a nice, even and smooth finish.

2 For each butterfly, use petal paste and small heart-shaped cutters in two different sizes to form the wings on each side.

3 Pipe the rest of the butterfly's body with royal icing and finish with small silver balls.

refreshing tip
Develop your springtime theme with other flora and fauna shapes, simply pressed out of coloured petal paste.

back to basics vanilla cupcakes p8... fondant icing p15... petal paste p16...

chocolate lover

Anyone with a sweet tooth will have fallen in love with a cake at least once in their lives, and will find themselves head over heels for the rich chocolate sponge and decadent frosting of these tempting cupcakes.

for 24 cakes...

- ♡ 1 batch of Not So Little chocolate cupcakes in red foil cases
- ♡ 1 batch of chocolate frosting
- ♡ large star-nozzled piping bag
- ♡ red sugar hearts
- ♡ red sugar sprinkles

1 Pipe the frosting in large swirls onto the cakes; make sure you do this slowly to ensure a generous portion on each.

2 Gently push a sugar heart into the top, just enough to secure it.

3 Add sprinkles around the heart, ensuring that plenty of the luscious chocolate frosting is still visible!

lovely idea
If you make these for a winter wedding, try using gold cases and sprinkles to give the rich chocolate a sumptuous shimmer.

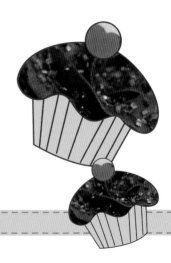

back to basics chocolate cupcakes p9... chocolate frosting p13...

engagement bling

You've a big event to celebrate so make an impact with this stunning yet simple design that is sure to be a big hit.

for 36 cakes...

- ♡ 1 batch of Little vanilla cupcakes in silver foil cases
- ♡ 1 batch of fondant icing
- ♡ small quantity of petal paste
- ♡ small circular cutters
- ♡ assorted sizes of silver or coloured ball decorations
- ♡ edible silver or gold paint
- ♡ edible glue

1 Carefully ice the top of each cake with a neat circle of fondant icing and allow to set. Take care not to make the mixture too thin.

2 Make the ring band out of thinly rolled petal paste, using two concentric circular cutters, and then paint with edible silver paint (or gold if you prefer).

3 Apply the ball decorations, securing in place with edible glue, to complete the ring.

engaging thought

This design is very colour versatile and can be easily adapted to co-ordinate with the colours of the real engagement ring!

back to basics vanilla cupcakes p8... fondant icing p15... petal paste p16...

black satin

Who would have thought a cupcake could remind you of sexy lingerie and black satin sheets! These scintillating cupcakes are bound to get you in the right mood to celebrate with that special someone.

for 36 cakes...

- ♡ 1 batch of Little vanilla cupcakes in red foil cases
- ♡ black ready to roll fondant icing
- ♡ royal icing
- ♡ pink colouring
- ♡ pastry cutter
- ♡ heart-shaped decorations and small silver balls
- ♡ small nozzled piping bag

1 First of all roll out black ready to roll fondant icing, cut out circles with a pastry cutter and then place on the cupcakes.

2 Mix royal icing with a little pink colouring to achieve a medium pink colour and then pipe three long thin lines.

3 Finish the design with alternating red hearts and small silver balls.

wedding bells
Create this design in pretty whites and pinks or blues for a more innocent take on the theme for a bridal shower.

back to basics vanilla cupcakes p8... royal icing p14... ready to roll icing p15...

more cupcakes for...

anniversaries

Celebrate these special wedding anniversaries with mouth-watering cupcakes personalised for the occasion.

first of many

This a paper anniversary, so why not use rice paper to create some heart-shaped decorations, but don't forget to make it 366 if it's a leap year.

sleek silver

Lengths of very thin rolled icing cut into strips like ribbon pasta, and beautifully decorated, can create a stunning effect for this all-important event.

tip to remember
Edible writing pens can sometimes be an easier option than piping. We used them on the 'first of many' cupcake (left).

ruby bubbly

The chink of glasses is always a nice way to celebrate. Capture the bubbliness of champagne with this design or choose different shapes of glasses or colours of drinks to match your favourite tipple.

bold gold

This truly memorable occasion is deserving of some pretty memorable cakes. When grouped together like this, metallic balls create real impact.

coa coa loco

A big splash of colour swimming in chocolate is the general idea here… chocolate drops, fruit candies and jelly sweets all work well to make a colourful display.

for 36 cakes...

- ♡ 1 batch of Little chocolate cupcakes in dark brown cases
- ♡ 1 batch of chocolate frosting
- ♡ palette knife
- ♡ plentiful supply of colourful chocolate or fruit sugar-coated sweets

1 Smooth a generous circle of chocolate frosting onto each cupcake and flatten into a very shallow swirl with a palette knife.

2 Separate out your coloured sweet decorations beforehand, particularly if you are making a lot of cupcakes, all with the same pattern.

3 Gently position the sweets into the arrangement of your choice.

bright idea
Leave the decorations to the last minute as some of them will absorb moisture and may lose their brightness or crumble if left too long before they're eaten.

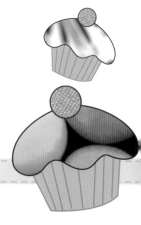

back to basics chocolate cupcakes p9... chocolate frosting p13...

1st birthday

A great way to mark your little one's landmark occasion… just say it with cupcakes.

for 36 cakes...

- ♡ 1 batch of Little vanilla cupcakes in red foil cases
- ♡ ½ batch of fondant icing
- ♡ ½ batch of royal icing
- ♡ food colouring
- ♡ thin nozzled piping bag

1 Carefully ice the top of several cupcakes with a neat circle of brightly-coloured fondant icing and allow to harden off for at least an hour.

2 Make the royal icing to the right consistency for piping letters and numbers. Pipe one per cupcake, and arrange on platters or tiers.

no.1 tip

If you have a mixed group of adults and children coming to the celebration, make up some larger cupcakes as well to match the designs of the smaller versions.

back to basics vanilla cupcakes p8... royal icing p14... fondant icing p15...

candy store

These irresistible treats conjure up wonderful images of candy shops… for you and the kids! This is one design you don't need to spend time carefully arranging.

for 36 cakes…

- ♡ 1 batch of Little vanilla cupcakes in brightly coloured cases
- ♡ 1 batch of buttercream frosting
- ♡ large star nozzled piping bag
- ♡ small fork
- ♡ buckets of your child's favourite mini sweets
- ♡ food colouring

1 Divide your frosting batch into smaller batches so you can make up several different colours.

2 Place a generous swirl of frosting on the cupcake and then scatter on the candy topping.

3 Use a small fork to work in some of the sweets and then scatter on a few more.

quick dip
Just tip their favourite miniature candies into bowls, turn your ready-frosted cupcake upside down and dip!

back to basics vanilla cupcakes p8… buttercream frosting p12…

make a face

Kids can join in or take the lead here... just set them up with lots of edible bits and pieces and some plain fondant iced cakes, they won't need much teaching to create scrumptious-looking smiley faces!

for 24 cakes...

- ♡ 2 batches of Not At All Little cupcakes in plain or pastel cases
- ♡ 2 batches of fondant icing
- ♡ icing colour
- ♡ quantities of sweets the kids can use to make eyes, noses, mouths, hair and so on

1 Prepare the face decorations. Be careful to avoid using anything children might possibly choke on.

2 Using the larger cupcakes allows children the most room to be creative. Spread a disc of fondant icing onto each cupcake, coloured enough to represent skin colour and set aside.

3 Round up the kids and, after giving them a short demonstration, retire to a safe place...

let's face it
It's probably a good idea to give each child their own little stock of items for face decorations.

back to basics vanilla cupcakes p8... fondant icing p15...

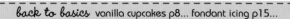

rocky mountain

Ideal for kid's bonfire nights and halloween parties, these look absolutely sumptuous and are bound to leave them all speechless... for a nice change!

for 24 cakes...

- ♡ 1 batch of Not So Little chocolate cupcakes in plain dark brown or brightly coloured cases
- ♡ 1 batch of chocolate frosting
- ♡ palette knife
- ♡ melted chocolate (dark or milk to your taste)
- ♡ mini marshmallows and popcorn

1 Apply a generous swirl of chocolate frosting to each cupcake and spread around with a palette knife.

2 Start building up your 'mountain of rocks' with an assortment of popcorn and marshmallows, securing them in the frosting as you go.

3 Finish with a generous drizzle of chocolate, and serve immediately.

rock solid tip

Although you can, of course, melt chocolate over the top of these – it's just as effective and much less bother to use the squeezy chocolate sauce but watch out for messy fingers!

back to basics chocolate cupcakes p9... chocolate frosting p13...

sugar and spice

These multi-coloured sweets are so versatile and can be sliced or broken into all kinds of shapes. Add a dusting of sugar to make the cupcakes shimmer and sparkle – these pretty creations are definitely what little girls are made of!

for 36 cakes...

- ♡ 1 batch of Little cupcakes in bright coloured cases
- ♡ 1 batch of butter-cream frosting
- ♡ knife
- ♡ an assortment of multi-coloured sweets, ready sliced or broken into different shapes
- ♡ coloured sugar sprinkles
- ♡ colouring

1 Cover each cupcake generously with tinted buttercream frosting and draw up into small peaks with a knife.

2 Press in and arrange sweets to make an attractive display of colour.

3 Finish off with a scattering of coloured sugar sprinkles.

oh so pretty

We've used pink and yellow coloured cases in the picture. Try a selection of the many pastel coloured cases now available for that extra touch of sweetness.

back to basics vanilla cupcakes p8... buttercream frosting p12...

more cupcakes for...

new arrivals

A new addition to the family is a real cause for a celebration! These unique cupcakes will be the talk of the party and will go perfectly with some champers to wet the baby's head.

new baby

A fitting way to celebrate such a wonderful event. These elegant little jewels in their individual gift boxes are a perfect choice gift for guests at christenings.

gift wrapped

Why not send your guests home with a cupcake favour bon bon. Wrap in circles of clear cellophane and tie off the top with ribbon.

celebrate the date

Look what the stork has brought! These delicate cupcakes mark that special occasion so beautifully and are a simple, yet so pretty way to celebrate your child's naming party. These look superb arranged on pastel china platters or tiers.

mother's day flowers

Mums around the world will really love these pretty cupcakes and they are bound to appreciate how much effort you have gone to for their special day.

for 24 cakes...

- ♡ 1 batch of Not So Little vanilla cupcakes in pretty coloured cases
- ♡ ½ batch of rose-coloured royal icing
- ♡ small quantity of petal paste
- ♡ 1 batch of buttercream frosting
- ♡ rose stencil
- ♡ palette knife
- ♡ round cutter
- ♡ rose-coloured sprinkles
- ♡ star nozzled piping bag

1 Pipe a generous swirl of buttercream frosting over each cupcake. Roll out a thin plaque of petal paste, large enough to make several roses at once and allow to harden off.

2 Make a stiff paste of rose coloured royal icing and, using a palette knife, spread into stencil while it is placed on the surface of the plaque. Lift the stencil off carefully.

3 Cut out roses with a round cutter and place two on the frosting. Finish with sugar or sprinkles.

mum's the word

For that extra bit of indulgence, try flavouring the frosting with a few drops of rose water after whisking.

back to basics vanilla cupcakes p8... royal icing p14... petal paste p16...

hats off to uncle sam

The 4th July is a day for family fun. Whether celebrating indoors or outdoors with fireworks and BBQ, these patriotic little cupcakes are sure to please.

for 36 cakes...

- ♡ 1 batch of Little vanilla cupcakes in red foil cases
- ♡ 1 batch of buttercream frosting
- ♡ icing tools or a sharp paring knife
- ♡ petal paste
- ♡ yellow sparkles
- ♡ coloured sugar strands
- ♡ edible glitter

1 Using a palette knife, spread a spoonful of yellow buttercream frosting right to the edges of each cupcake.

2 To make the hat, start with the shape in white and then build the colours on top – first the red stripes and then the blue band and the white star.

3 Finally add glitter to the hat and coloured sugar strands and sparkles to the frosting.

independent thought
Stick a miniature indoor sparkler in some of the cupcakes and turn off the lights (don't leave unattended).

back to basics vanilla cupcakes p8... buttercream icing p12...

the graduate

It's an important time in any young person's life – wherever they are graduating from, it's your chance to show them how proud you are of their achievements.

for 24 cakes...

♡ 1 batch of Not So Little vanilla cupcakes in plain or foil cases

♡ ½ batch of roll icing

♡ ½ batch of coloured ready to roll fondant

♡ white petal paste

♡ edible ink pen

♡ star sprinkles

1 Spread a smooth neat disc of coloured fondant to the edges of the cake.

2 Roll out a thin ribbon of red fondant and place on the cake to look like untied ribbon.

3 Make a diploma scroll from very thinly rolled petal paste and use an edible ink pen to write the name. Write the words on the scroll before you roll it up and place it on the cake, it's a lot easier. Place on fondant and finish with a few star sprinkles.

first class
Practice writing with the ink pen before trying it on the scroll, as it can be fiddly.

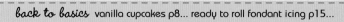

back to basics vanilla cupcakes p8... ready to roll fondant icing p15...

thanksgiving treats

Make sure you have all got room after the turkey for these fruity treats. Give thanks for the harvest by creating these sweet little cakes for the whole family.

for 12 cakes...

- ♡ 1 batch of 12 Not At All Little vanilla cupcakes
- ♡ a tin of Morello cherries drained or fresh cherries, stoned
- ♡ cherry glaze
- ♡ icing sugar for dusting
- ♡ double cream
- ♡ piping bag and nozzle

1 Remove the tops of the cakes, taking a deep circular groove of cake sponge with them and set aside.

2 Place the cherries in a little pile in the centre of each cupcake and then spoon over the cherry glaze while it is not quite set.

3 Replace the cake tops, shaving some of the cake off underneath so they sit nicely on top. Dust the cupcakes with icing sugar then finish with a swirl of double cream.

harvest display
Try other ideas, such as apple pie filling or any seasonal berries in jam.

back to basics vanilla cupcakes p8...

halloween headline

Never mind the usual ghosts and pumpkins, they will take their hats off to you over these! There is very simple modelling involved in these spooky specimens so you can be as creative as you like.

for 24 cakes...

- ♡ 1 batch of Not So Little vanilla cupcakes in orange or halloween cupcake cases
- ♡ ½ batch of fondant icing
- ♡ black and red rolled fondant icing
- ♡ bright yellow
- ♡ star sprinkles
- ♡ piping nozzle
- ♡ glitter

1 Spread a plain white fondant icing disc over each cupcake, close to the edges. Using a suitable size piping nozzle and the black rolled fondant, fashion the cone of the witch's hat around the nozzle, allowing enough excess to make the floppy brim.

2 Put a thin red band of rolled fondant icing around the base of the hat.

3 Decorate the hat with several stars and finish with a scattering of glitter.

spooky thought
Try your newfound modelling skills with other shapes… black cats, broomsticks and cauldrons.

back to basics vanilla cupcakes p8... fondant icing p15...

new year, new cupcake

When the clock strikes 12, make sure you have a glass of champagne to hand, as well as one of these delightful celebratory cupcakes.

for 24 cakes...

- ♡ 1 batch of 24 Not So Little vanilla cupcakes in silver coloured cases
- ♡ 1 batch of rolled fondant, coloured blue
- ♡ small amount of petal paste
- ♡ edible silver paint
- ♡ glitter

1 Apply a smooth disc of blue rolled fondant to each cake to make the face of the clock.

2 Cut small strips of thin petal paste and coat with silver paint to make the dial of the clock and the hands pointing to midnight.

3 Finish with multi-coloured glitter.

ring the changes
They don't have to be all the same – use different coloured fondant, chocolate or coffee sponge and bright cases so everyone can choose a different one.

back to basics vanilla cupcakes p8... petal paste p16...

more cupcakes for...

springtime

Easter is the perfect occasion to create some scrumptious tea-time treats which are tasty and look gorgeous too!

easter bunny

A cute cupcake with little bunnies peeking out will go down a storm with guests.

in bloom

A lovely way to enhance that springtime feeling when Easter arrives! Try different colour combos too.

cheep trick

If you are really short of time, there are some great Easter sprinkles now available, little chicks and Easter bunnies, all in lovely pastel colours.

in the nest

A traditional favourite – but make sure you make enough because everyone will want at least one!

duck pond

Kids will love these 3-D cupcakes with a cute little trail of ducklings following behind.

tea for two

A traditional design for a very traditional occasion, but these cakes have extra indulgence of icing on the cake as well as cream and fruit below – pure heaven!

for 24 cakes...

♡ 1 batch of Not So Little vanilla cupcakes in plain or silver foil cases

♡ ½ batch of fondant icing

♡ double cream – whipped

♡ fresh summer berries

♡ sprinkles to co-ordinate with the fruit

1 Spread a neat circle of fondant close to the edge of each cupcake, leaving a border. Allow to harden, covering with sprinkles when almost dry.

2 Cut a complete circle of cake out of the top of the cake, creating a hollow. Cut the removed cake in two and set aside.

3 Place a generous dollop of cream in each crater and embed a few berries in the cream. Replace the two halves to make butterfly wings and finish with more sprinkles.

dainty idea

Make up a medley of different berries to put in each cupcake.

back to basics vanilla cupcakes p8... fondant icing p15...

hot stuff

Looking just like miniature BBQs themselves, these hot little numbers will go as quickly as hot potatoes... so make sure you make plenty of them! Fiery orange sweets and coal-black biscuits work best.

for 24 cakes...

- ♡ 1 batch of Not So Little chocolate cupcakes in dark brown cases
- ♡ 1 batch of chocolate frosting
- ♡ honeycomb and biscuits, broken into chunky pieces
- ♡ sharp knife
- ♡ jelly sweets

1 Spread a base of chocolate frosting onto each cupcake, sufficient to provide a bed for the topping.

2 Arrange broken pieces of honeycomb and biscuits to create a 'hot coals' effect. For breaking the biscuits neatly, use a sharp knife. Despite the use of a knife you don't get clean edges (which you don't want anyway) but you do get pieces of the right size rather than a load of crumbs.

3 Finish with a few jelly sweets (the most orangey ones in the packet) amongst them to look like flames.

hot tip

Add fruit on cocktail sticks to look like fruit kebabs on the barbie.

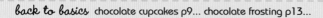

back to basics chocolate cupcakes p9... chocolate frosting p13...

dressed for dinner

Your guests will be shaken, if not stirred, by these magnificent after dinner treats. Suitable for both Bonds and Miss Moneypennys.

for 24 cakes...

- ♡ 1 batch of Not So Little vanilla cupcakes in plain or foil cases
- ♡ 1 batch of white rolled fondant icing
- ♡ black petal paste
- ♡ small pearl and silver balls
- ♡ brush

1 Spread neat circles of white fondant icing – alternatively, choose whatever colour suits your colour theme – and allow to dry.

2 Make the bow ties and handbags by cutting out of thinly rolled and pre-coloured rolled fondant.

3 Apply to fondant disc on top of each cake with a damp brush. Finish by adding three pearl balls for the men's bow ties and silver and a white ball for the ladies' handbags.

perfect host
Place the cupcakes in individual boxes as place settings too.

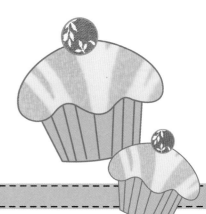

back to basics vanilla cupcakes p8... rolled fondant icing p15...

double trouble

Everyone will get a big surprise when they bite into these and see the two colours of the sponge inside. Try all sorts of colour combinations for creative results. Finish with co-ordinating coloured sweets for a young at heart look.

for 24 cakes...

♡ 1 batch of Not So
   Little vanilla cake
   mix divided into two

♡ food colouring

♡ 1 batch of
   buttercream frosting

♡ multi-coloured
   sweets

1 Divide cake mix in two and colour both halves with contrasting food colouring. You will have to use a lot to ensure the colours stand out.

2 Spoon in the cake mix into baking cases, but in two halves, side by side.

3 When baked and cooled, decorate in swirls or peaks with buttercream frosting. Finish with a generous covering of multi-coloured sweets.

that's magic
Always use natural
food colouring as you
will need to use a lot
for bright colours

back to basics cupcakes p8... buttercream frosting p12...

coffee morning treat

Worth breaking the diet for, these indulgent delights are topped with meringue and sprinkled liberally with two tone chocolate flakes... delicious!

for 24 cakes...

- ♡ 1 batch of Not So Little coffee cupcakes in patterned cases
- ♡ 1 batch of meringue
- ♡ cappuccino chocolate for grating
- ♡ café curls
- ♡ cocoa powder

1 Smooth a generous layer of whipped meringue over the top of each cupcake and place under the grill for a few seconds until the meringue has browned on the surface.

2 Allow to cool and then sprinkle shavings of cappuccino chocolate on top and dust with cocoa powder. Finish with half a café curl and serve immediately with your favourite cup of coffee.

meringue mix

To make enough meringue to cover these cupcakes, you will need 3 egg whites, 175g (6oz) caster sugar, 5ml (1 tsp) cornflour, 2.5ml (½ tsp) vinegar and 2.5ml (½ tsp) vanilla. Beat the egg whites until very stiff. Then gradually beat in the sugar, cornflour, vinegar and vanilla. Then spread the meringue in peaks over the cupcakes and place under the grill long enough to turn the surface peaks golden brown.

back to basics coffee cupcakes p9...

ice cream picnic

When is an ice-cream not an ice-cream?... when it's one of these neopolitan delights! You'll have great fun making these two-tone toppings and all the family will be so impressed.

for 24 cakes...

- ♡ 1 batch of Not So Little vanilla cupcakes in pretty patterned cases
- ♡ 1 batch of buttercream frosting, split into two for colouring pink and green
- ♡ big star nozzled piping bag
- ♡ colourful sprinkles
- ♡ ice cream wafers

1 The two-tone effect is achieved by filling the piping bag with two different colours of frosting. It's a bit tricky to get the two colours side by side in the icing bag and may take a bit of practice. You must also use quite a big bag and nozzle.

2 Fill one side of your icing bag with one of the colours of frosting. Turn the bag around and carefully fill the other half of the bag with the second colour. Make a generous two-tone swirl on each cupcake, as you would make a normal swirl. Finish with multi-coloured sugar or chocolate strands and wafers.

ice idea
Try flavouring the frostings e.g. with strawberry and mint for that extra special treat.

back to basics vanilla cupcakes p8... buttercream frosting p12...

more cupcakes for...

special birthdays

You only have the 'big' birthdays once so make sure they go with a bang with fabulous cupcakes.

sweet sixteen

These sweets, cut thinly in cross section, make a lovely colourful display for the youngsters.

eighteen today

This is a very versatile idea – you can use little or even 'petit four' size cupcakes to create any word or number, or theme the colours all gold or silver for example.

twenty one

Very minimalist but incredibly striking when all grouped together. Make sure you have enough cakes though! Repeat patterns regularly to create a designer effect.

love-forty

Candles on picks look great – forty should be fun after all! Cut the numbers out of petal paste, and for the best effect match the colour to the colour of your cupcake case.

oriental charm

'3 in 1' pagoda cupcakes are a lot of fun, easy to make, and will particularly appeal to those members of the family with a hearty appetite!

for 24 pagoda cakes...

♡ 1 batch of Not So Little vanilla cupcakes in gold foil cases

♡ 1 further batch of vanilla cupcake mix to split between Little and Very Little

♡ gold foil cases

♡ 1 batch of fondant icing, coloured red

♡ gold sparkle dust

♡ angelica

1 Spread a neat circle of coloured fondant icing onto the top of each size of cupcake.

2 Before the icing hardens off too much, carefully stack the cakes on top of each other to create your pagoda.

3 Finish by making a roof effect with strips of angelica.

4 Finally, scatter a little gold sparkle dust on the exposed icing.

pile up

Try different coloured foil cases – red, silver and green are readily available – to make a multi-coloured display.

back to basics vanilla cupcakes p8... fondant icing p15...

island paradise

You can just imagine yourself stretched out on this idyllic little scene, lying under a parasol with your flip flops kicked off…

for 24 cakes...

- ♡ 1 batch of Not So Little vanilla cupcakes in plain cases
- ♡ 1 batch of buttercream frosting, coloured golden yellow
- ♡ small amount of petal paste
- ♡ blue and green colouring
- ♡ orange sugar
- ♡ cocktail umbrellas
- ♡ shiny cake decorating dragees/balls

1 Start your beach scene by covering each cupcake with yellow buttercream frosting.

2 Sprinkle lightly with orange sugar to complete the sunny effect.

3 Cut out sandals from coloured rolled petal paste, and then make very thin strips for the thongs.

4 Finally complete the toe decoration with a single same colour shiny dragee and finish with a cocktail umbrella.

sandy tip
Make some variations to this – e.g. comb the frosting or make little hills in it to look like sand dunes.

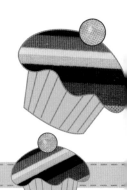

back to basics vanilla cupcakes p8... buttercream frosting p12... petal paste p16...

80   dream themes

singing star

Go on, show off your talents with these star quality designs... These cute cakes are sure to hit the right note.

for 24 cakes...

- ♡ 1 batch of Not So Little vanilla cupcakes in plain cases
- ♡ 1 batch of white fondant icing
- ♡ 1 batch of royal icing, coloured black
- ♡ thin nozzled piping bag
- ♡ yellow/gold stars

1 Spread a neat disc of white fondant icing onto each cupcake.

2 When the icing has set a little, pipe the musical staves, notes and treble clef onto the cupcakes.

3 Finish with yellow stars on and around the musical staves.

star turn

Instead of piping, cut out musical shapes and stars from rolled petal paste. You could even make a more 3-D effect by placing them upright in frosting rather than icing.

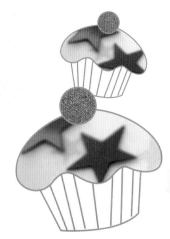

back to basics vanilla cupcakes p8... royal icing p14... fondant icing p15...

bollywood beauty

Bring a touch of Eastern magic to your cake decorating with this eye-catching paisley design made up of lots of non-pareils and dragees.

for 24 cakes...

- ♡ 1 batch of Not So Little vanilla cupcakes in gold foil cases
- ♡ 1 batch of fondant icing coloured pastel pink
- ♡ gold dragees/balls
- ♡ orange and pink non pareils
- ♡ piping nozzle
- ♡ small quantity of royal icing with pink colouring
- ♡ cocktail sticks

1 Make your paisley shape in paper first, to fit the size of the cupcake top and place on the surface. Trace the outline with a cocktail stick, and then pipe a very thin line of pink royal icing along the outline.

2 Before the piping sets, fix the small gold dragees along the piping line. Repeat the above with the inside paisley pattern shape.

3 Fill in the area inside the gold balls with pink non-pareils. Lightly dampen the icing first with a brush so they will stay in place. Fill the middle with orange non-pareils and add a large gold ball in the centre.

spice it up...
Try adding spice into the cake mix, all spice, for example, just ½ tsp per batch.

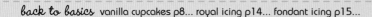

back to basics vanilla cupcakes p8... royal icing p14... fondant icing p15...

pop your cork

These have a real celebratory feel to them and should definitely be served with champagne too!

for 24 cakes...

- ♡ 1 batch of Not So Little vanilla cupcakes in gold foil cases
- ♡ 1 batch of buttercream frosting
- ♡ small gold balls/dragees
- ♡ edible gold leaf
- ♡ edible gold paint
- ♡ edible glue
- ♡ petal paste
- ♡ green colouring
- ♡ cocktail sticks

1 Cover cakes in a thick layer of frosting and finish in small peaks. Colour petal paste to the colour of a champagne bottle and fashion a bottle top half.

2 Hollow out the neck with a cocktail stick, paint with edible gold paint and finish with gold leaf. Press at an angle into the centre of the frosting.

3 Using edible glue, place some gold balls down the neck of the bottle. Finish by scattering little gold balls or dragees over the buttercream.

bright ideas...
Different colours can be used to good effect here – pink cases and frosting for pink champagne; gold for Bucks Fizz etc.

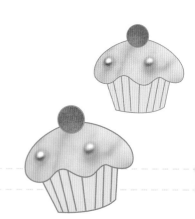

back to basics vanilla cupcakes p8... buttercream frosting p12...

retro look

Even your cupcakes have to keep up with the latest fashion trends… and this dates back to '60s monochrome looks. Fortunately, minimalist designs are 'in' right now so they're not too difficult to reproduce!

for 24 cakes...

- ♡ 1 batch of Not So Little vanilla cupcakes in silver foil cases
- ♡ 1 batch of white rolling fondant icing
- ♡ 1 batch of black rolling fondant icing
- ♡ fondant rolling pin
- ♡ board
- ♡ set each of pastry and small circular icing cutters
- ♡ sharp knife
- ♡ apricot glaze

1 Firstly, create a nice smooth flat surface to your cupcakes by shaving or slicing off any lumps or bumps with a sharp knife.

2 Apply a light apricot glaze to the surface of the cupcakes so the fondant top you make will stick to it. Make the pattern to your own style, by rolling out the fondant and cutting out different circles and circle rings, interchanging them and pressing in lightly.

3 When your pattern is finished, use a circular cake cutter of the right diameter to cut out a finished top for your cupake.

retro style
For a funky pattern, alternate black and white stripes.

back to basics vanilla cupcakes p8... fondant icing p15...

more cupcakes for...

show stopping outfits

The most important part of getting ready for a party is your outfit. Accessorise with these sweet treats.

awesome accessory

Use a piece of red rolling fondant just like modelling clay to make your handbag design and bling it up with shiny decorative balls.

dancing shoes

Trace and cut your shoe shapes out of rolled coloured fondant or, if you can, make them more 3-D to match the handbag. Use plenty of sugar sprinkles to make them really stunning.

bling bling
Paint your decorations with edible glue and glitter to make a large variety of sparkling and colourful baubles for a cake with pizazz.

edible undies
Once you have your basic pants and bustier shapes cut out of fondant, use edible pens and glitter and your imagination to create some lovely patterns and designs. The button on this one has been made by dipping a pearl ball in edible glue and then rolling in glitter!

wedding wonders

shabby chic

Whoever said romance was dead? These sweet little pink hearts are actually really easy and create a vintage romantic setting for the day.

for 24 cakes...

♡ 1 batch of Not So Little vanilla cupcakes in silver foil cases

♡ 1 batch of buttercream frosting

♡ petal paste

♡ food colouring

♡ pink sanding sugar

♡ heart-shaped cutters

1 Roll out a piece of coloured petal paste, large enough to make quite a few hearts from the one piece. Using a cutter, make the hearts well in advance and allow to harden.

2 Make frosting and pipe a generous swirl over each cupcake.

3 Place two hearts at different angles into the frosting swirl and finish with a sprinkle of pink sanding sugar.

chic to chic

You could always pipe your bride and groom initials on each heart to add that final romantic touch.

back to basics vanilla cupcakes p8... buttercream frosting p12... petal paste p16...

spring fresh

These cute butterfly designs will give your wedding day that fresh springtime feel and will complement the sunny weather you have specially ordered for the day.

for 36 cakes...

- ♡ 1 batch of Little vanilla cupcakes in coloured cases
- ♡ 1 batch of fondant icing
- ♡ pastel green and pink colouring
- ♡ petal paste
- ♡ small silver balls
- ♡ small amount of royal icing and colouring
- ♡ thin piping nozzle
- ♡ heart-shaped cutters, two different sizes

1 Spread a smooth neat disc of pastel-coloured fondant icing to the edges of the cakes and allow to set.

2 Roll out a piece of pale pink petal paste thinly and use two different sizes of heart-shaped cutters to make the wings.

3 Place wings on each cake and, using a thin nozzle, pipe the body and antennae with royal icing.

4 Finish the tips of the antennae with silver balls.

flutter by
Use flower cutters
for a country
garden theme.

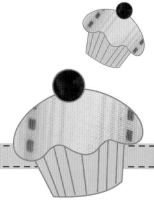

back to basics vanilla cupcakes p8... fondant icing p15...

daisy chain

These cute cupcakes look so indulgent, but they are really simple to make and your guests will absolutely love them.

for 24 cakes...

- ♡ 1 batch of Not So Little vanilla cupcakes in gold foil cases
- ♡ 1 batch of butter frosting
- ♡ small amount of white petal paste
- ♡ daisy cutter
- ♡ coral non-pareils
- ♡ edible gold paint
- ♡ coral decorative sugar
- ♡ star nozzled piping bag
- ♡ fondant rolling pin
- ♡ glitter

1 Make butter frosting and, using a star nozzle and bag, pipe a generous criss-cross swirl (rather like a plait) on each cupcake. Roll out a thin piece of white petal paste, press out daisies with a cutter and allow to harden.

2 Brush the centre of the daisy with edible glue and place five or six of the coral non-pareils in the middle of each daisy. Brush the petals with gold paint and sprinkle glitter on them while still damp.

3 Place the daisies on the cupcakes. Finish off by sprinkling with coral decorative sugar.

colour swatch

These gorgeous cakes also look fab when contrasted with silver daisies.

back to basics vanilla cupcakes p8... buttercream frosting p12... petal paste p16...

chocolate radiance

So informal, yet so temptingly delicious! These fab cakes will look absolutely gorgeous on the day. You'll have to be quick to make sure you get one before they all disappear!

for 24 cakes...

- ♡ 1 batch of Not So Little chocolate cupcakes in dark brown cases or dark patterned cases
- ♡ 1 batch of chocolate frosting
- ♡ selection of chocolate cigarillos
- ♡ white chocolate vermicelli
- ♡ star nozzled piping bag

1 Make chocolate frosting and pipe a generous swirl on each cupcake. Make sure there is enough that the cupcake looks really luscious.

2 Next, arrange a selection of varied chocolate cigarillos, like criss-crossed logs, on top of the cupcake.

3 Add a light sprinkle of gold glitter to match the gold in the cases or non-pareils to match the colour of the patterned cases, Finish with a scattering of white chocolate vermicelli (optional).

grate idea
Grate plain, milk or white chocolate bars instead.

back to basics chocolate cupcakes p9... chocolate frosting p13...

rosebud romance

Always the choice for the timeless traditional wedding. What's more, these days, there is an astonishing array of beautiful handmade roses, now easily available from any cake decorating or craft store.

for 24 cakes...

♡ 1 batch of Not So Little vanilla cupcakes in red foil cases

♡ 1 batch of vanilla buttercream frosting

♡ large size pre-made petal paste roses or rose buds

♡ star nozzled piping bag

1 Make up some vanilla frosting. For a wonderful added touch, add some rose essence to the frosting. Pipe a generous swirl on each cupcake.

2 Carefully embed one rose into the centre of each cupcake.

3 Stand back and admire.

4 As an alternative, try lavender cases with a sprig of fresh lavender on top.

get real
Decorate the tables with real rose petals for a romantic effect.

back to basics vanilla cupcakes p8... buttercream frosting p12...

bridal tower

Cupcakes on a stacking tier with a small top bride and groom cutting cake to match are fast taking the place of traditional wedding cakes. It's easy to see why, when they look so stunning.

for the cutting cake and stacking cupcakes...

- ♡ 7.5 inch cake liners and 8 inch cake tin for the cutting cake
- ♡ cupcake tier in rigid acrylic or plastic or glass
- ♡ buttercream frosting
- ♡ lilac colouring
- ♡ petal paste
- ♡ silver glitter
- ♡ edible silver paint
- ♡ lilac sugar
- ♡ very large star and large star nozzles
- ♡ heart cutter

The cutting cake

For the cutting cake: make a 6oz, 3 egg cupcake batch. Mix and bake all the ingredients as a conventional cake, but in a liner so that when cooked (40–45 minutes on 160°C/320°F/gas mark 3), it will resemble a giant cupcake. Decorate the cutting cake and the cupcakes in exactly the same style, starting with a big lilac swirl of frosting. Make the hearts with cutters out of rolled out petal paste, and allow to harden. Brush the hearts both sides with edible silver paint and drench with glitter. Position the hearts all over the cakes and sprinkle the frosting with lilac sugar.

The cupcakes

Make enough batches to allow one Not So Little or two Little cupcakes per guest. Following the photograph, decorate the cupcakes in exactly the same way but on a much smaller scale!

back to basics cupcakes p8... buttercream frosting p12...

more cupcakes for...

wedding favours

Wedding favours are a time-honoured tradition and, with these cute cupcakes, they will be the talking point of the day.

white wedding

Match the colour of the cake with your outfit and accessories for a stylish coordinated look. These traditional white cupcakes in classic ivory boxes with complementary ribbon trimmings will even match your dress!

pretty pastels

Add a touch of glamour to your wedding with a carefully chosen favour box to complement your cupcake embellishments. A stylish satin rose and sleek silver box enhances these delicate pink cakes and will really impress your guests. Alternatively, a pretty pastel favour box will simply add elegance to any colour scheme,

105

first frost

Fans of 'minimalist chic' will love these stylish white, blue and silver cupcakes. Just make your cakes small and bite-sized to avoid un-stylish crumbs!

for 48 cakes...

- ♡ 1 batch of Very Little vanilla cupcakes in plain cases
- ♡ 1 batch of white fondant icing
- ♡ blue icing
- ♡ rolled blue petal paste
- ♡ reindeer and snowflake cutter (or the shape of your choice)
- ♡ silver edible dragees

1 Carefully cover each cake with a cap of white fondant icing. For this look, take a little extra time to ensure a crisp, clean finish around the edge.

2 For the snowflakes and reindeer, press your shapes from rolled blue petal paste. Use a cocktail stick to help remove the shapes intact from their cutters.

3 Once dry, place them onto the cakes. If necessary, use a drop of watery icing sugar to help them bond. Gently press a silver bead into the centre of the star.

cool tip
Try white frosting with blue sprinkles, as shown, for the same look – fast.

back to basics vanilla cupcakes p8... petal paste p16...

christmas morning

These stylish Christmas tree designs almost look like a bit of modern art – and you only need to learn how to pipe a squiggly line.

for 36 cakes...

- ♡ 1 batch of Little vanilla cupcakes in plain cake cases (or Christmas design cake cases)
- ♡ 1 batch of fondant icing
- ♡ royal icing
- ♡ green and red colouring
- ♡ fine nozzled piping bag
- ♡ yellow star-shaped decorations

1 Spread a smooth, neat disc of white fondant icing to the edges of the cakes and allow to set.

2 Colour your royal icing until you have the right 'Christmas green' colour and then pipe the tree in a continuous zig-zag line, starting from the top.

3 Finish with a blob of red royal icing for the base and a yellow star sprinkle for the top.

festive bonus
Have a go piping a holly leaf, a bell or a Christmas present.

back to basics vanilla cupcakes p8... royal icing p14... fondant icing p15...

tied up with ribbon

Bright and bold – these designs are striking and very versatile for many other gift occasions besides Christmas.

for 24 cakes...

- ♡ 1 batch of Not So Little vanilla cupcakes in red foil cases
- ♡ 1 batch of white fondant icing
- ♡ pink and red colouring
- ♡ rolled fondant icing
- ♡ pink confetti decorations
- ♡ red non pareils

1 Spread a smooth, neat disc of pale pink fondant icing to the edge of the cupcakes.

2 Roll out and cut strips of red fondant and lay across cupcakes to make a loose unknotted bow. Cut the ends of each strip into a 'V' for effect.

3 Finish with confetti sprinkles to enhance the decorative effect of the bow and then sprinkle with red non-pareils on to the pink icing to represent the design of the wrapping paper.

christmas tip
Dust the board lightly with icing sugar before rolling out your fondant.

back to basics vanilla cupcakes p8... fondant icing p15...

mistletoe kisses

These will be a lot of fun over the festive season. The idea is to lift up the little mistletoe plaque off the cupcake to get your Christmas kiss first. That's really having your cake and eating it!

for 24 cakes...

- ♡ 1 batch of Not So Little vanilla cupcakes in green foil cases
- ♡ 1 batch of buttercream frosting
- ♡ fine star nozzled
- ♡ piping bag
- ♡ petal paste
- ♡ mistletoe stencil
- ♡ small quantity of royal icing
- ♡ green colouring
- ♡ rolling pin
- ♡ palette knife
- ♡ mother of pearl decoration balls

1 Roll out the petal paste and cut out small squares, or different shapes if you like, and allow to harden off.

2 Place mistletoe stencil on each petal paste plaque and apply a small quantity of stiff green royal icing across the stencil with a palette knife to create the mistletoe picture.

3 Pipe a generous swirl of frosting on each cupcake. Place plaques on the cupcakes and complete with mother of pearl decoration balls for the mistletoe berries.

make a wish
If you don't have a stencil, pipe a twig of mistletoe with royal icing.

back to basics vanilla cupcakes p8... buttercream frosting p12... petal paste p16...

we three kings

These could well be the shining stars in your Christmas cupcake display — almost as precious as gold, frankincense and myrrh themselves!

for 24 cakes...

- ♡ 1 batch of Not So Little vanilla cupcakes in gold foil cases
- ♡ 1 batch of royal icing with a variety of colours
- ♡ 1 batch of fondant icing
- ♡ small nozzled piping bag
- ♡ shiny decoration balls
- ♡ shiny glitter

1 Prepare all the cupcakes with the three contrasting colours of icing, spreading a neat disc to the edge of each cupcake.

2 Choosing one colour at a time, pipe the coloured crowns on to each cupcake (try practising on a plate first).

3 Finish with shiny balls and glitter.

star tip
Recreate the starry night with this colourful shooting star design.

back to basics vanilla cupcakes p8... royal icing p14...

perfect present

This is a nice idea for simple Christmas presents or token gifts and you can make several at a time out of a batch of 48 cupcakes...

for 48 cakes...

♡ 1 batch of 48 Very Little vanilla cupcakes in a mixture of cases

♡ 1 batch of white fondant icing

♡ small quantity of petal paste

♡ several colourings

♡ shape cutters for bells, stars, baubles and candles

♡ small cake boxes, about 10cm x 10cm x 6cm, preferably with a window lid

♡ white tissue and cellophane

1 First, spread a neat disc of white fondant icing to the edge of all your cupcakes and leave to harden off a little. Make the traditional Christmas decorative shapes – ideally from cutters pressed out of coloured petal paste. If you don't have them make your own, tracing round with a sharp knife.

2 Place the shapes on the icing to suit the different coloured foil cases and finish with a brushing of edible glue and glitter. Arrange an assortment of the different decorations into boxes of four, using the cellophane and tissue to present the cupcakes and cushion them in their box.

in the bag
Use clear or foil printed cellophane bags or boxes instead.

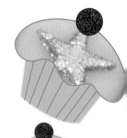

back to basics vanilla cupcakes p8... fondant icing p15...

more cupcakes for...

kid's christmas

These easily decorated cupcakes are ideal in the run up to the festivities – no need for cutting out shapes from icing.

pick up a penguin
You should be able to find many inexpensive yuletide cake decoration motifs readily available in supermarkets in the run up to Christmas.

polar bear
Transparent glitter gives a great polar arctic feel to these comical cakes.

sparkle and shine

Using glitter is a great way to add a magical snowy feel to cakes.

teddy bear

These could hardly be quicker to prepare – just select some co-ordinating non-pareils or glitter for a nice finishing touch.

mr frosty

White sanding sugar really enhances this snowman scene, and the Christmas cupcake case designs are perfect.

acknowledgments

Our thanks in particular go to Ming Yee Shiu, our daughter Sophie, and our son Nigel, for their enthusiastic support and encouragement and practical help in setting up our website and kick starting our cupcake business. Many thanks also to everyone at David & Charles – especially to Jenny Fox-Proverbs, for first suggesting to us that we should write this book.

suppliers

UK

Edsol Party Supplies
Edsol House
Buslingthorpe Green
Meanwood Road
Leeds L37 2HG
Tel: 01132 621122
www.edsol-party-supplies.com

Splat
P.O.Box 83
Princes Risborough
HP27 9WB
Tel: 0870 766 8290
www.splatcooking.net

Squires Group
Squires House
3 Waverley Lane
Farnham
Surrey GU9 8BB
Tel: 0845 225 5671
www.squires-group.co.uk

US

Candyland Retail Store
201 W. Main Street
Somerville
NJ 08876
Tel: (908) 685 0410
www.candylandcrafts.com

New York Cake Supplies
56 West 22nd Street
New York, NY – 10010
Tel: 800 942 2539
www.nycake.com

Wilton
Wilton Industries
2240 W. 75th Street
Woodridge, IL 60517
Tel: 630-963-1818
www.wilton.com

about the authors

Joan and Graham Belgrove left behind their careers in management and consultancy to launch The Little Cupcake Company Ltd in 2006 in response to the growing demand for unique celebration cupcakes. They now have an established internet business supplying cupcakes nationally to both private customers and major companies.

www.thelittlecupcakecompany.co.uk

index